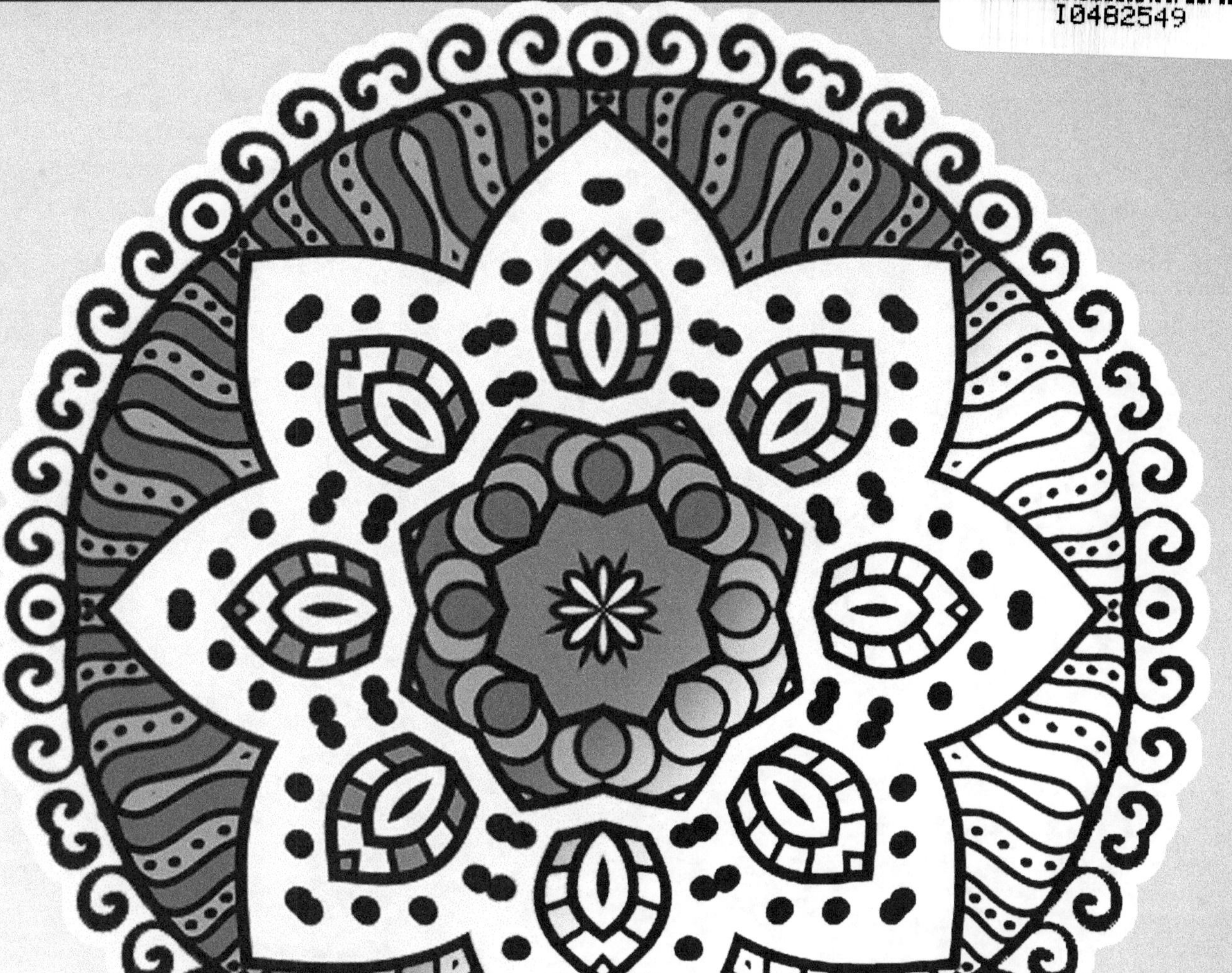

WONDERFUL MANDALA

MANDALA COLORING BOOK

COLOR TEST PAGE

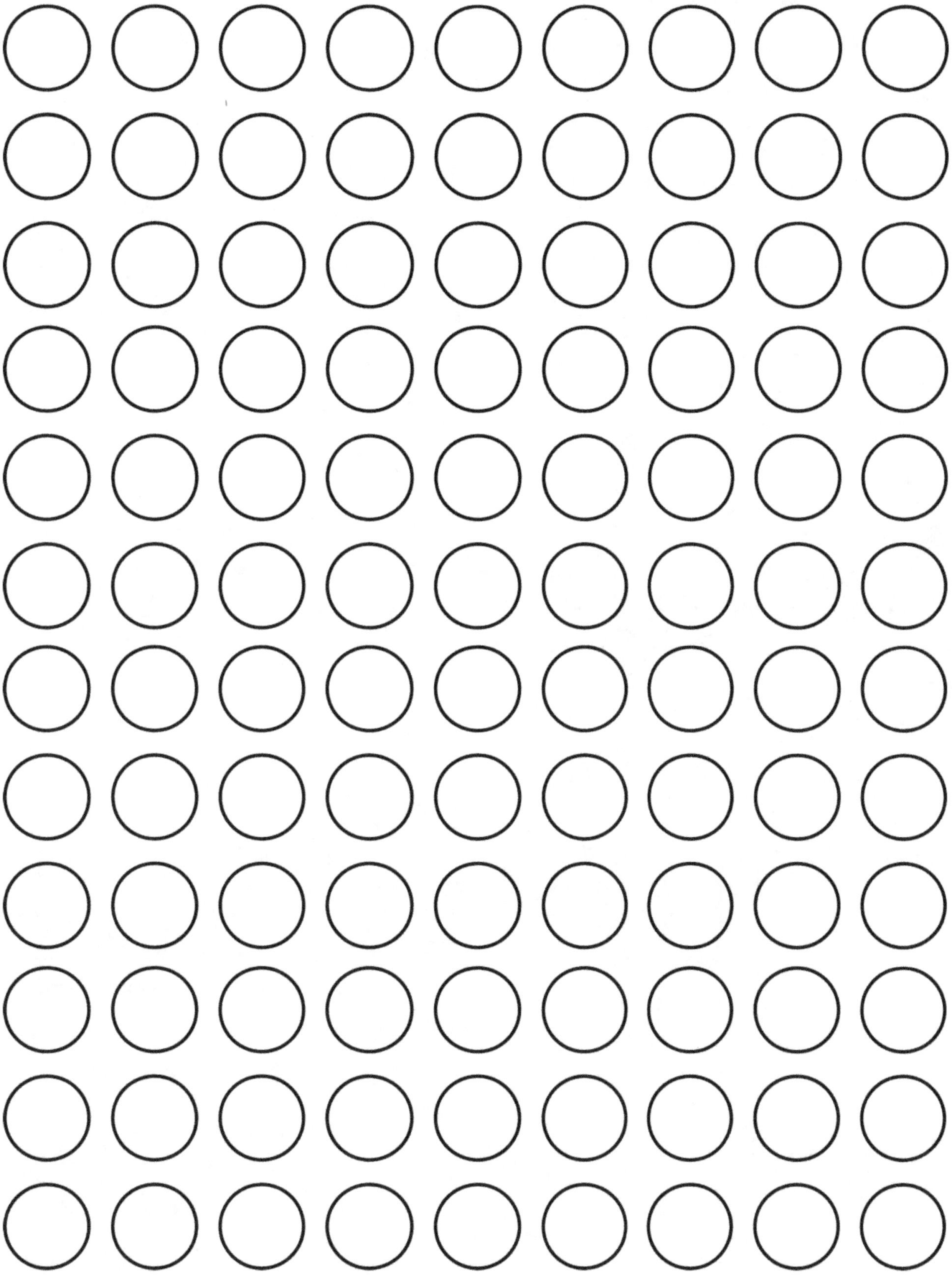

COLOR TEST PAGE

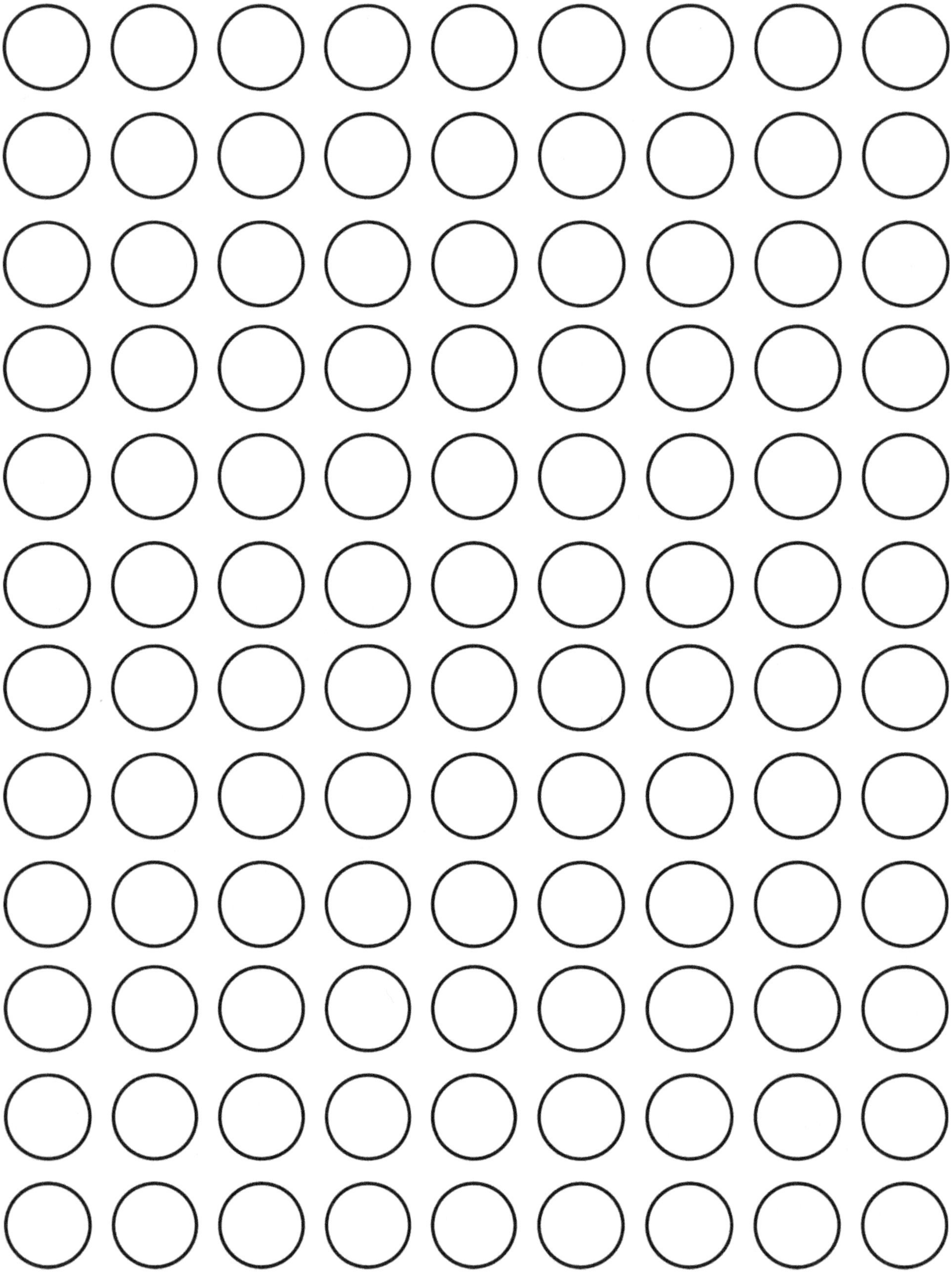

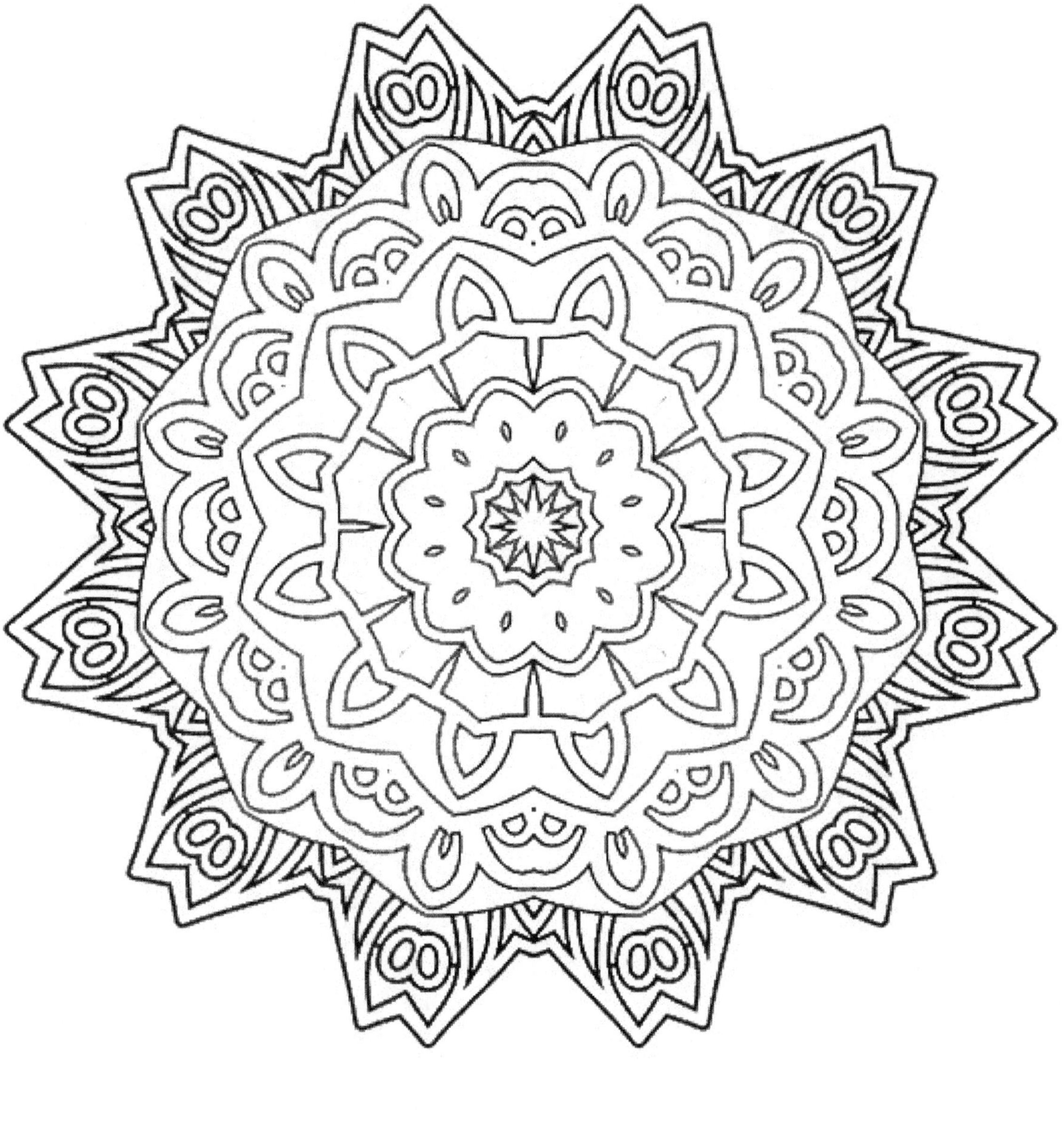

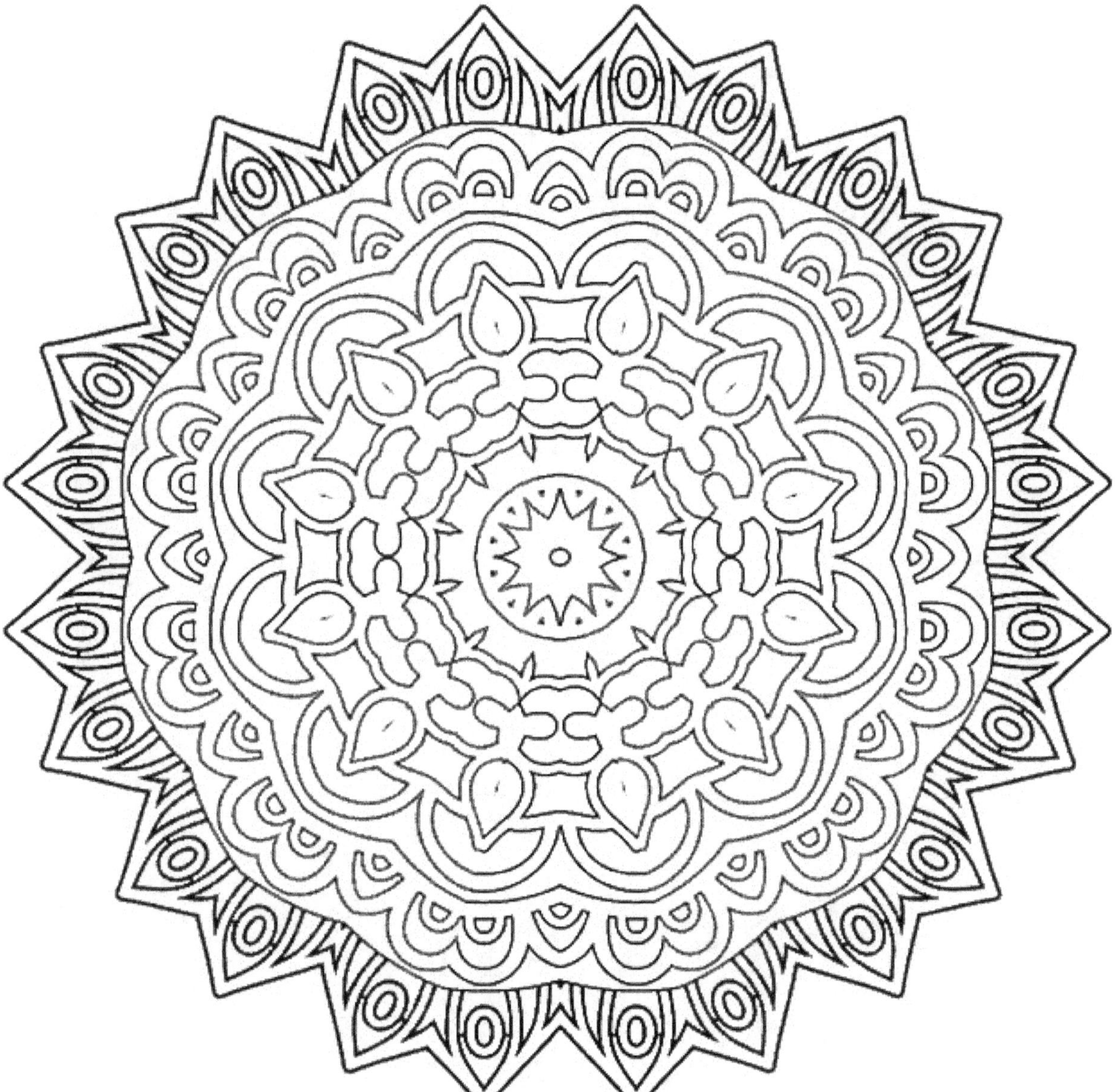

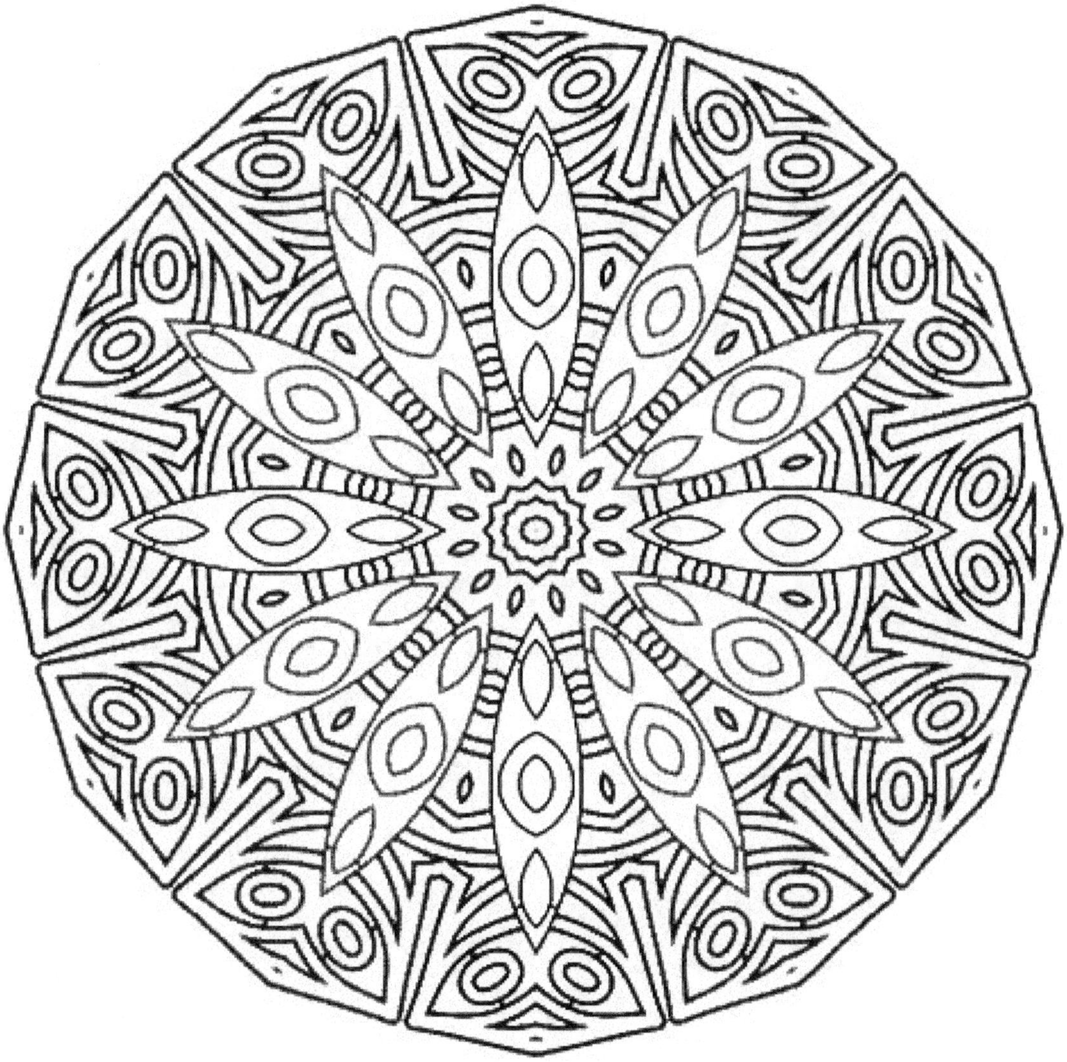

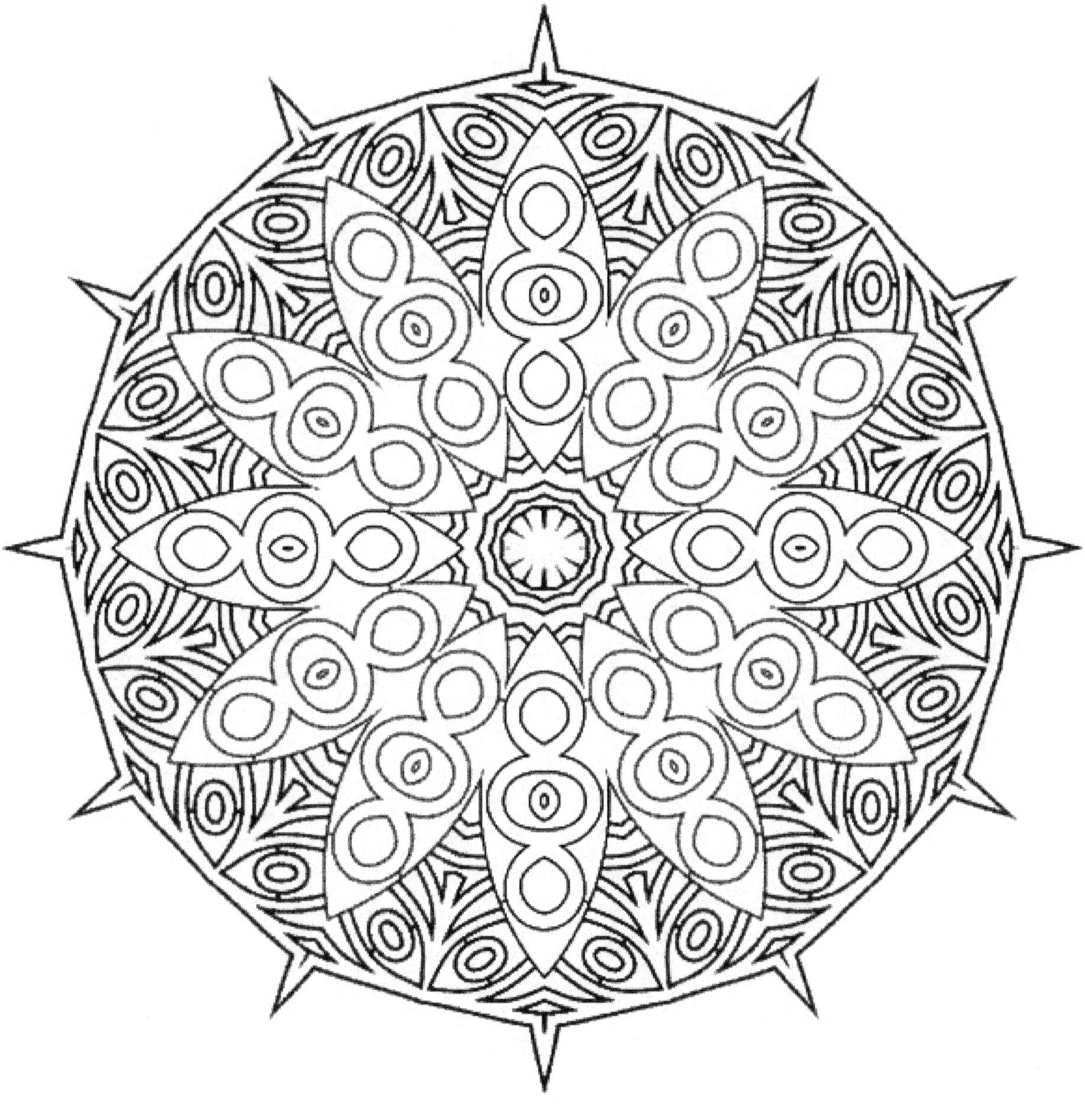

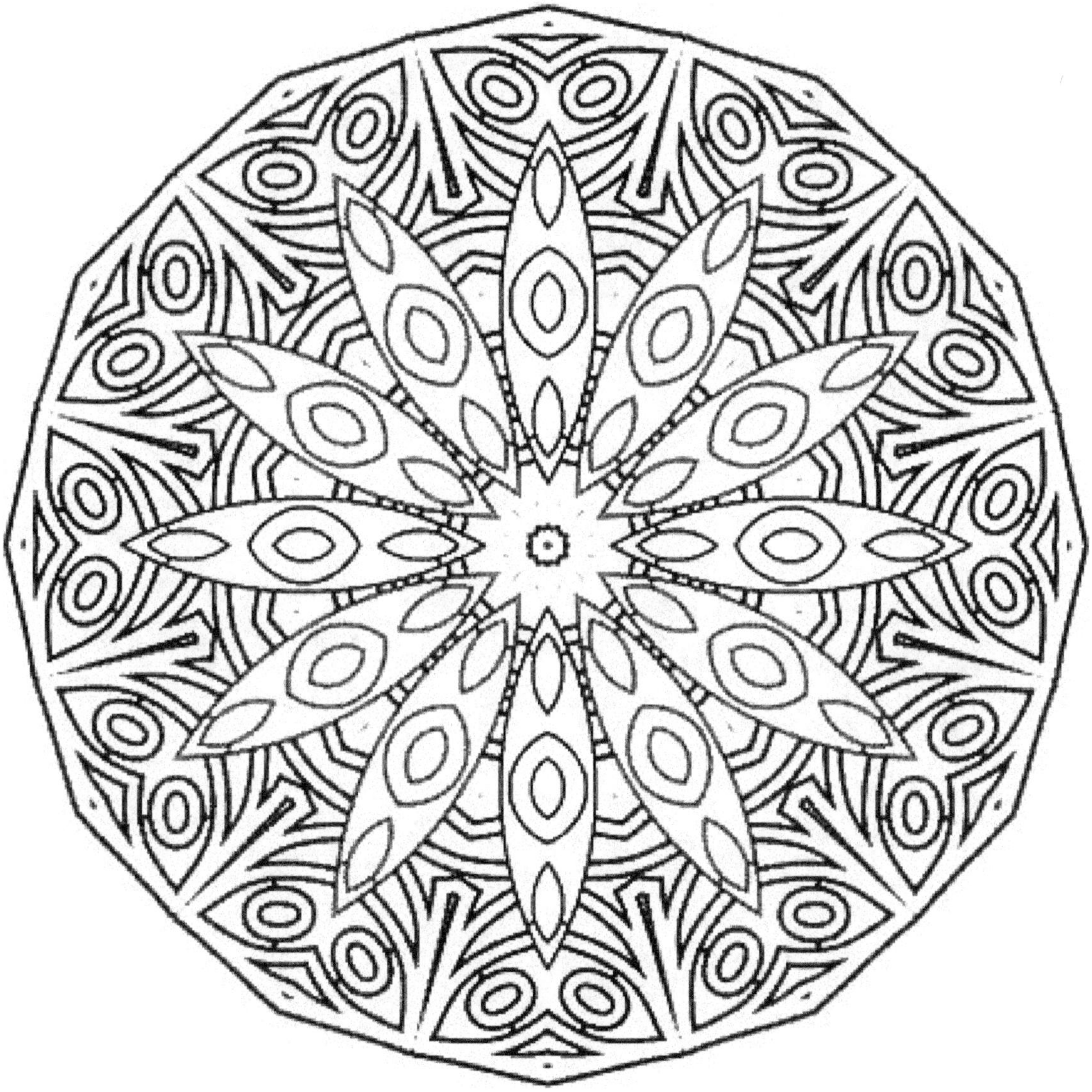

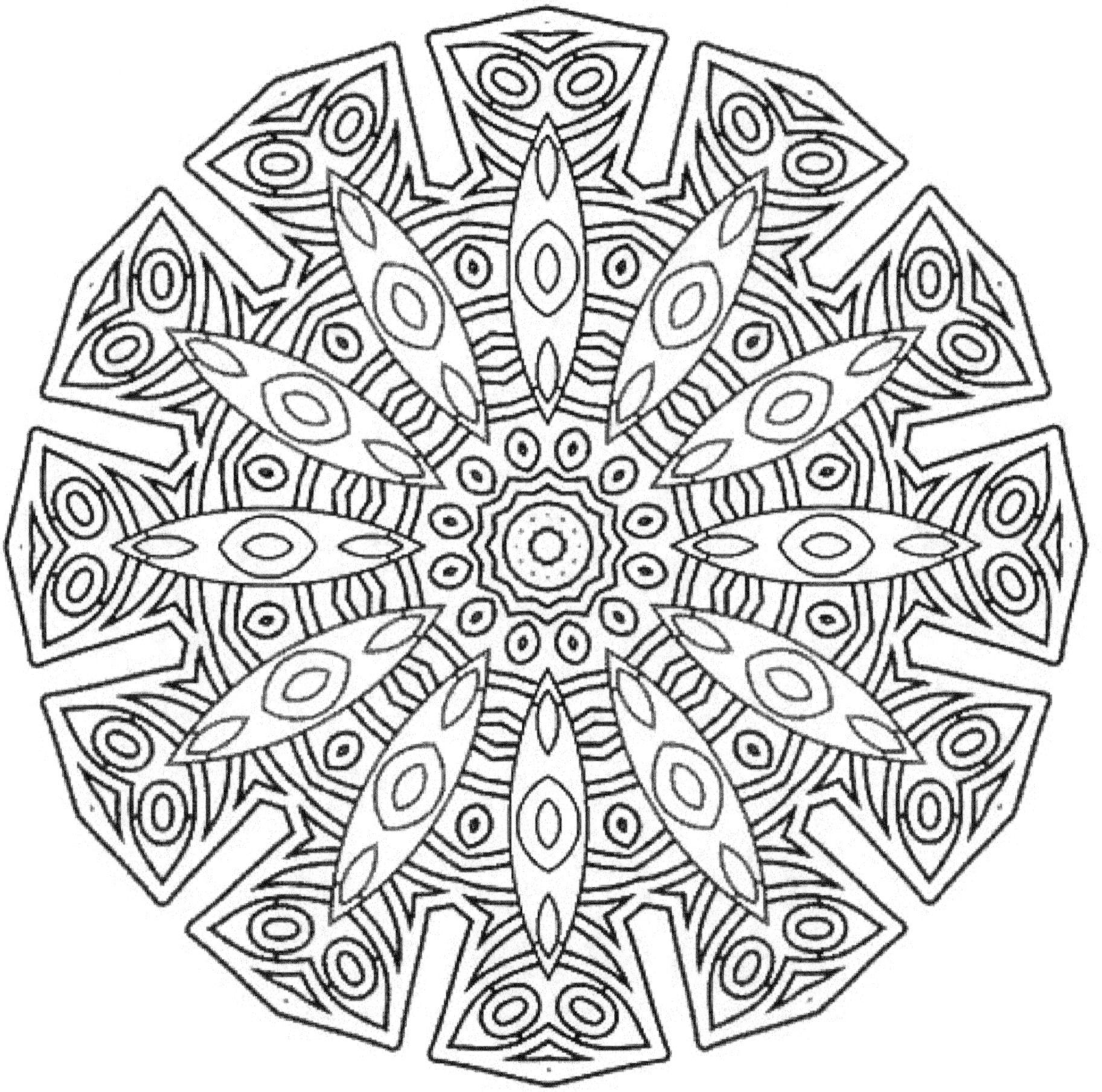

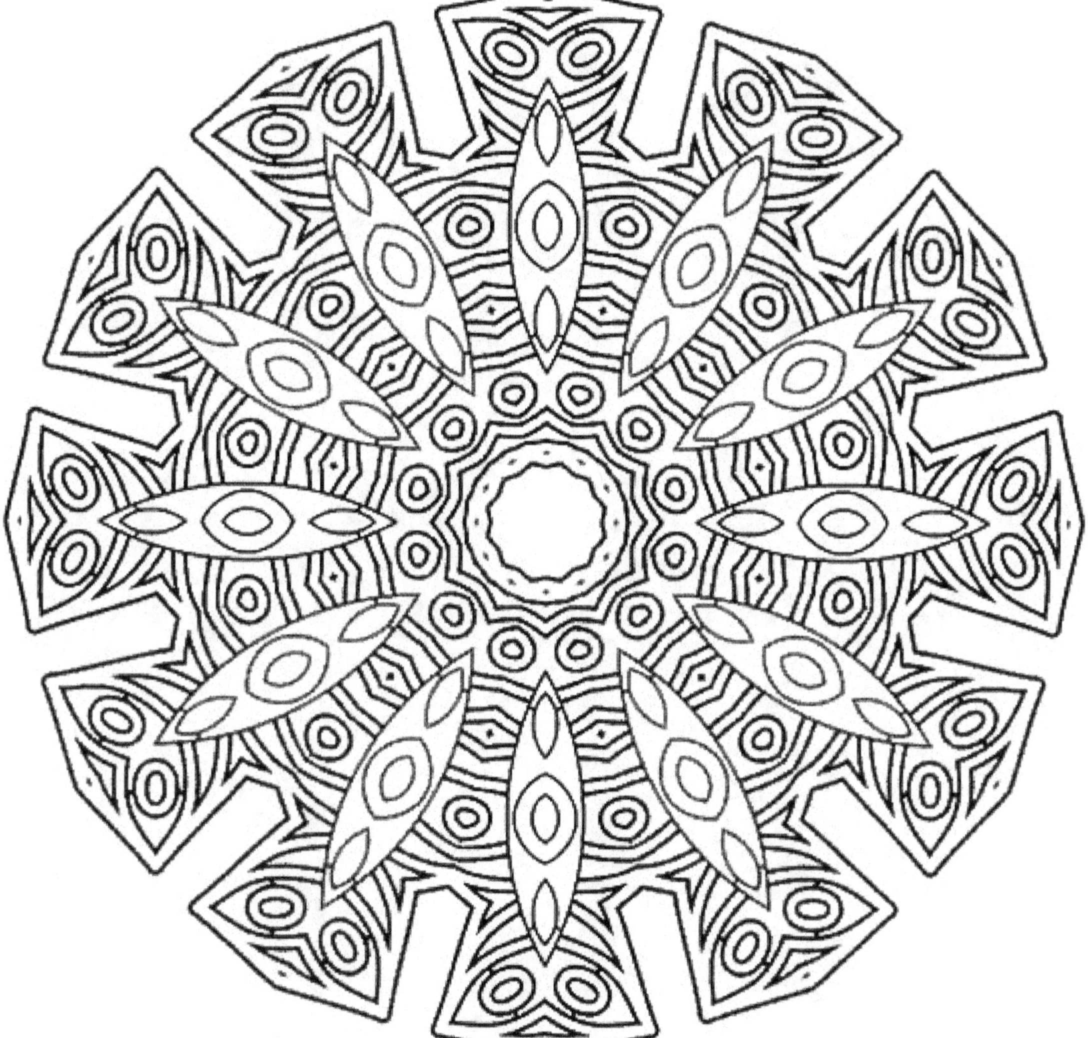

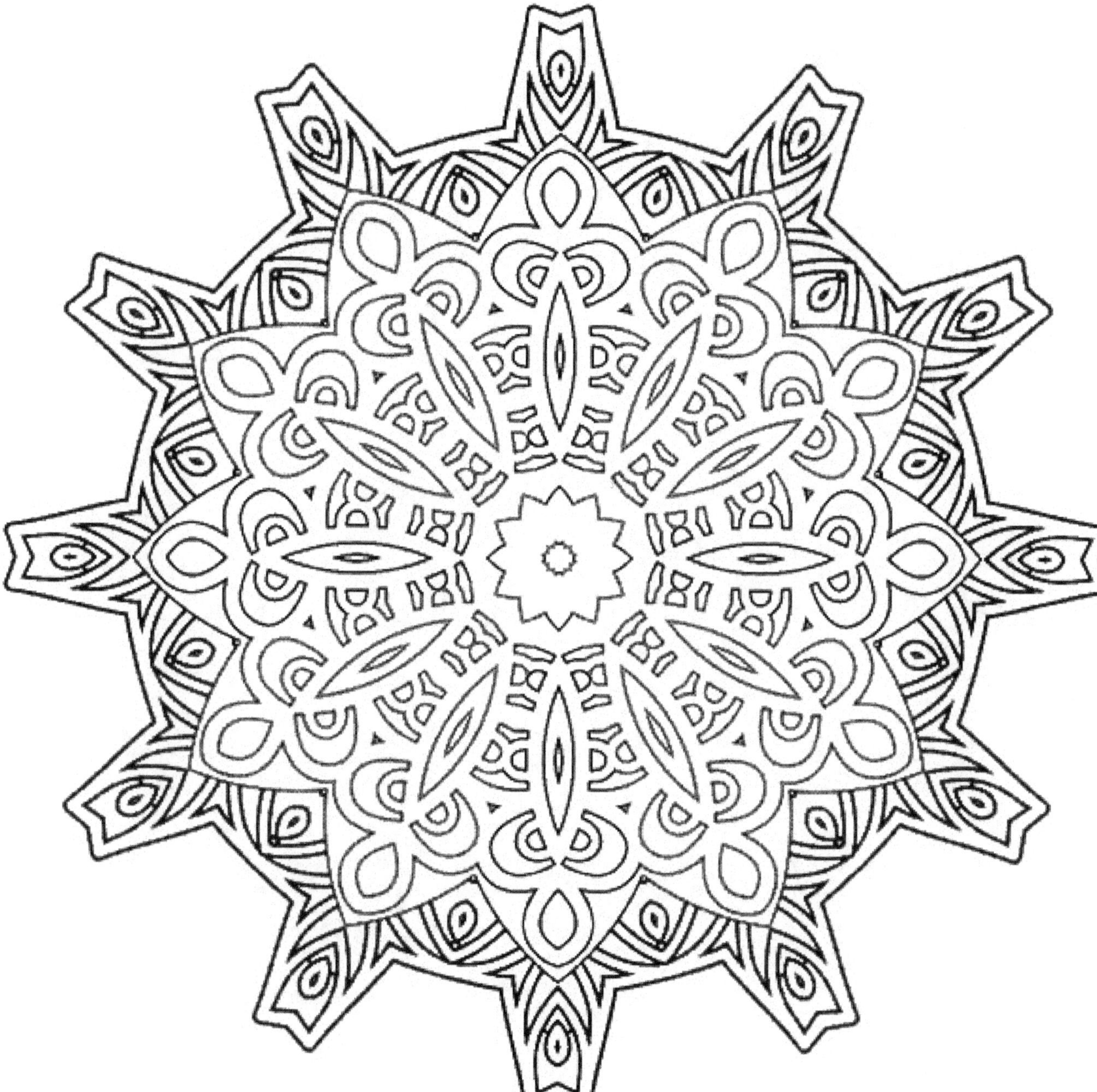

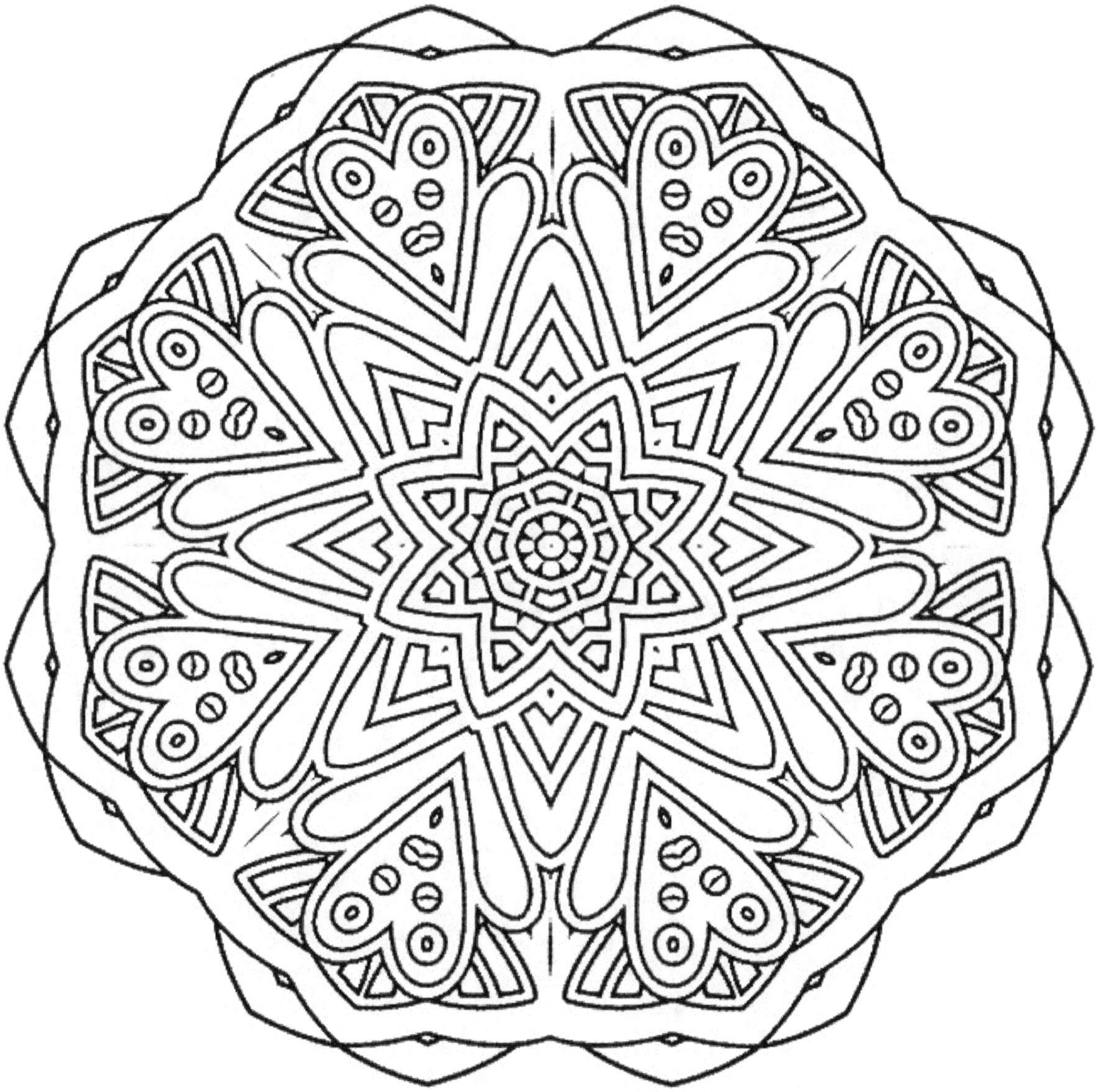

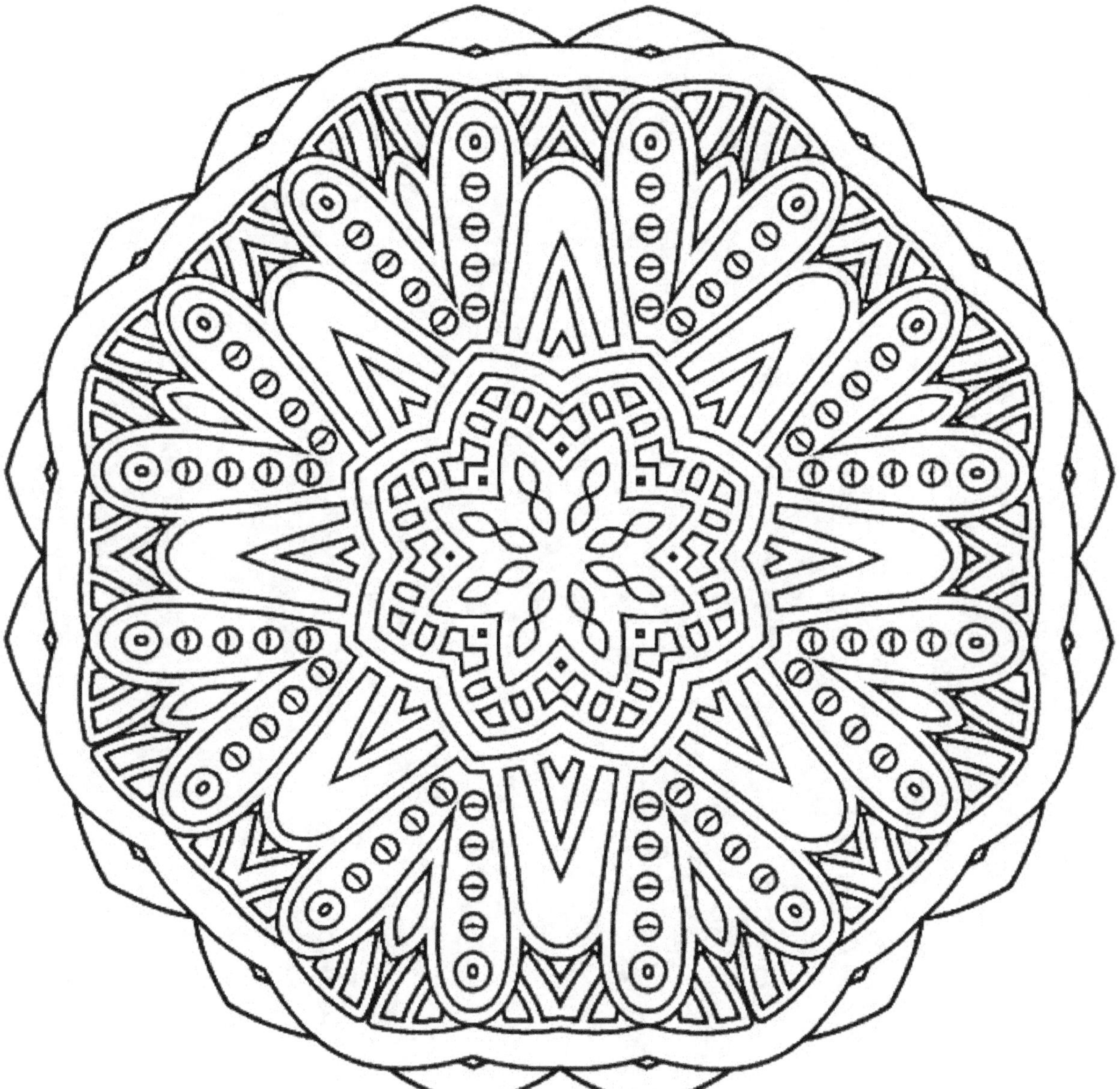

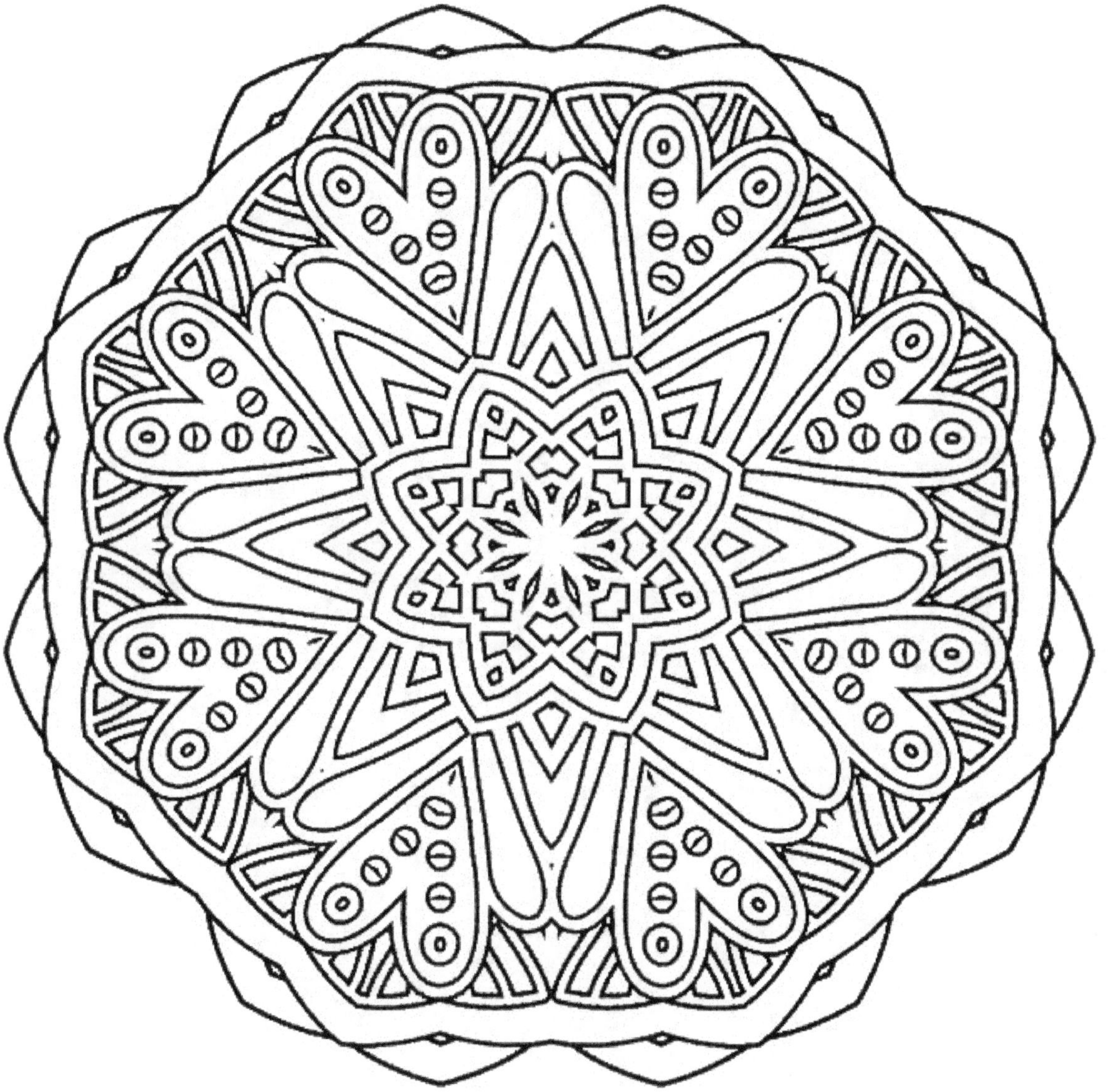

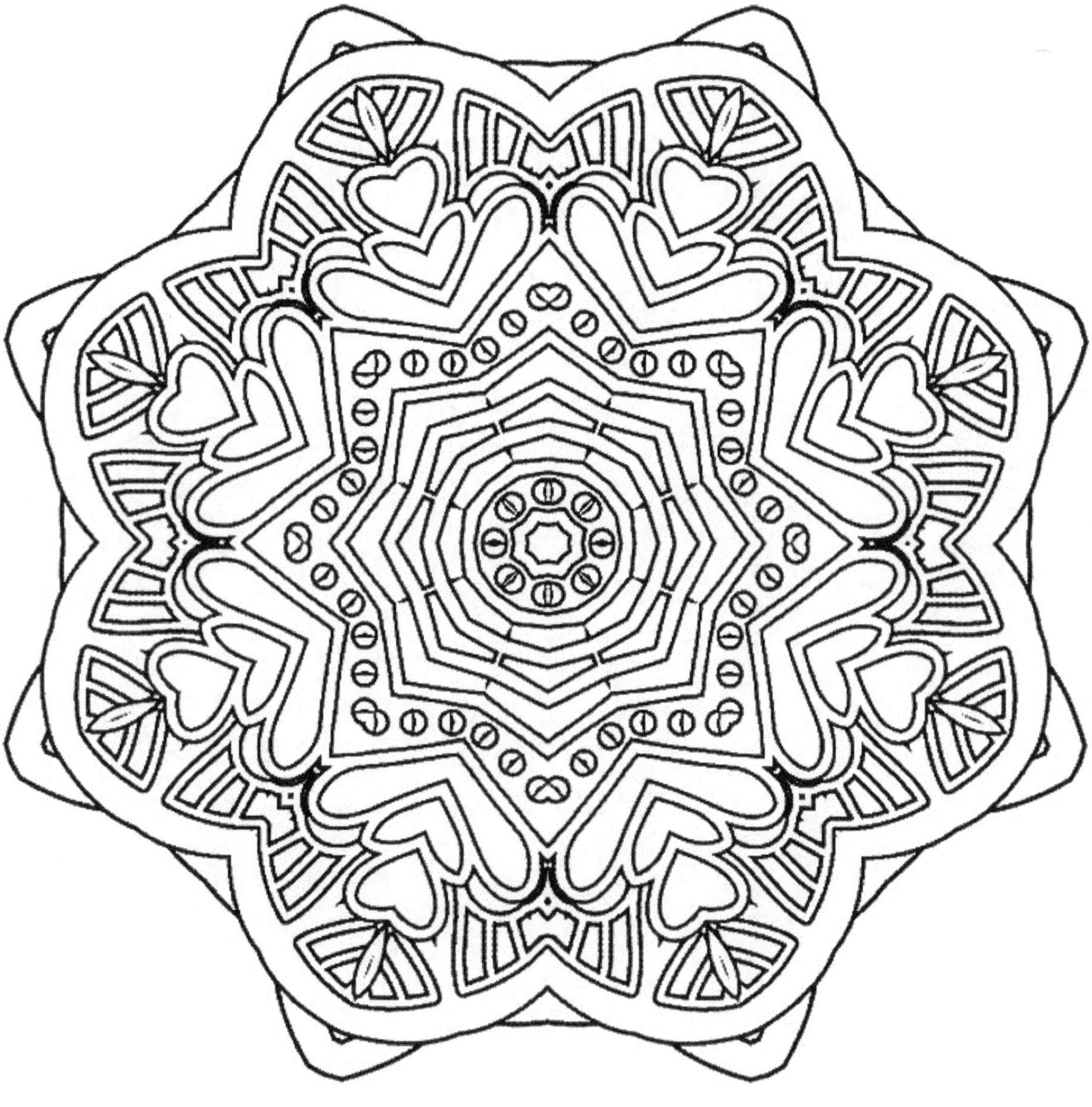

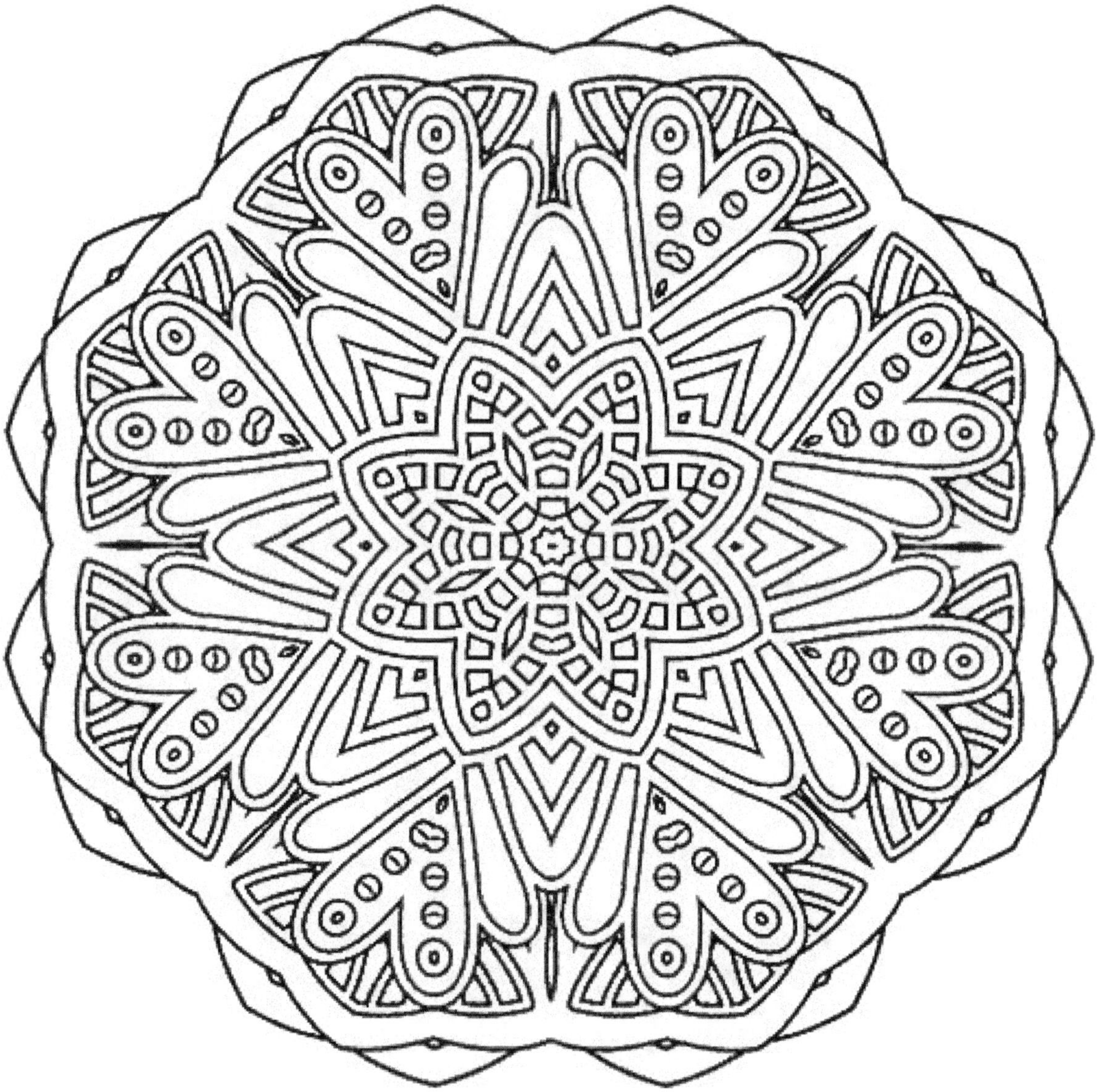

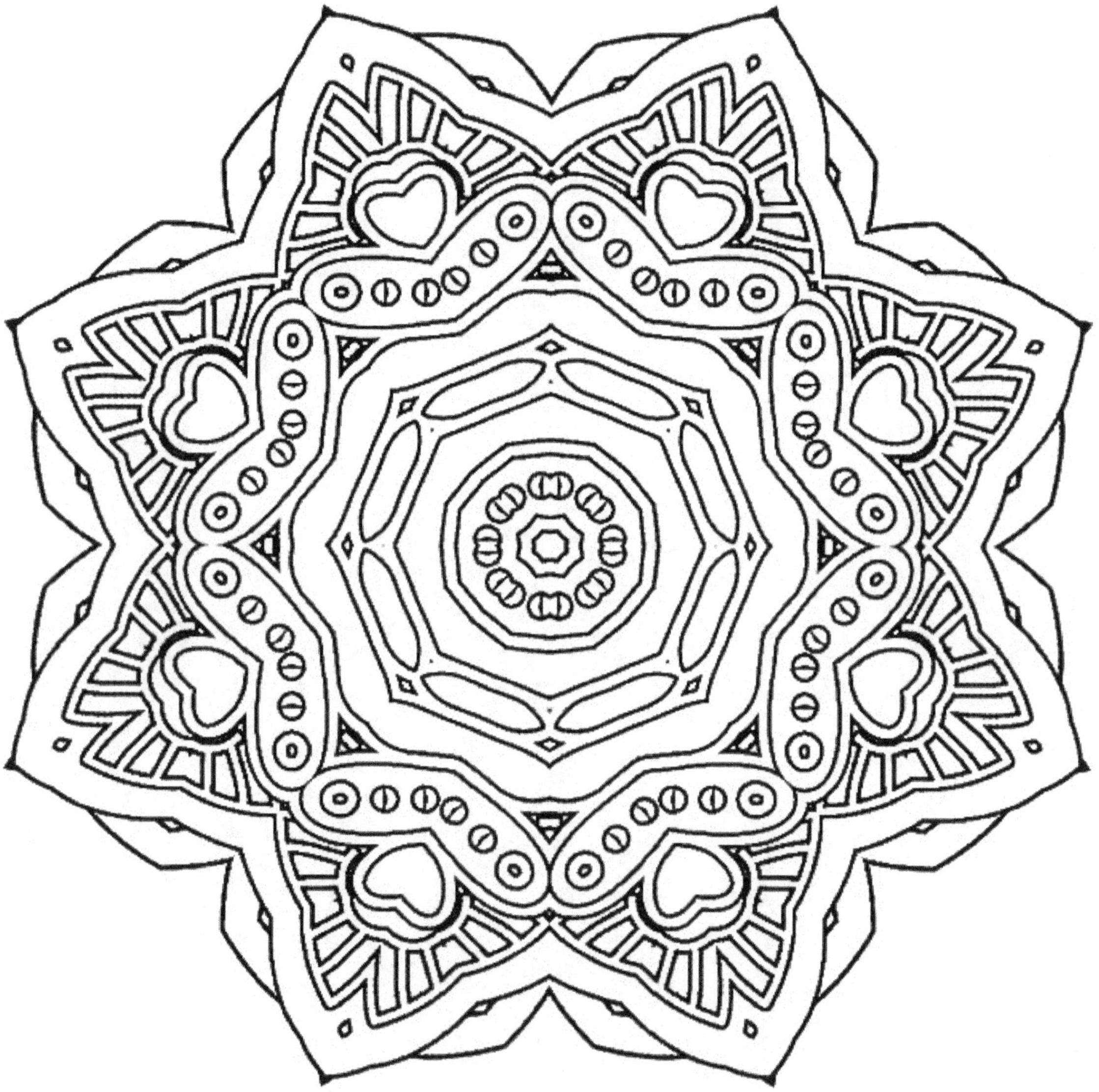

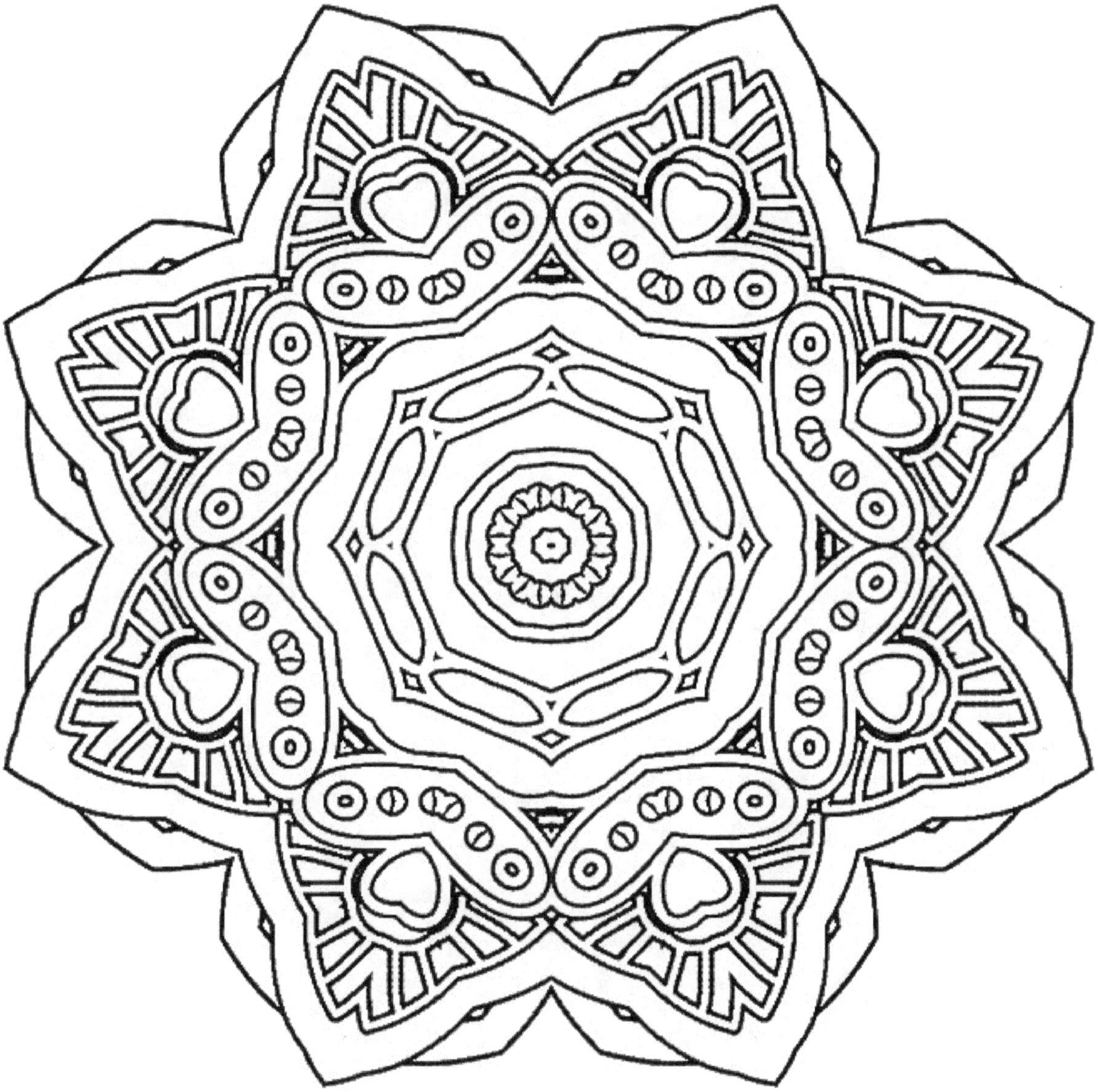

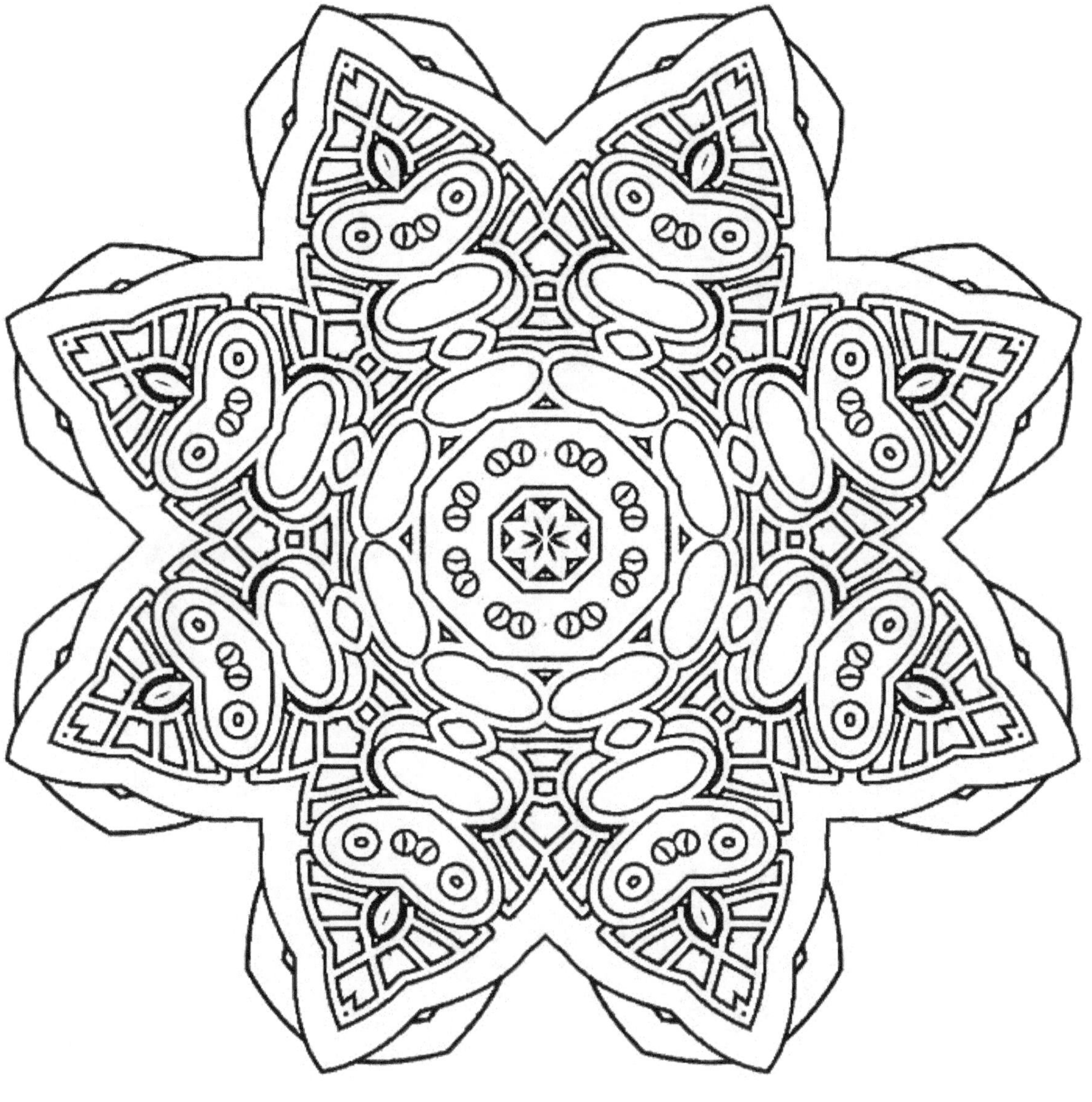

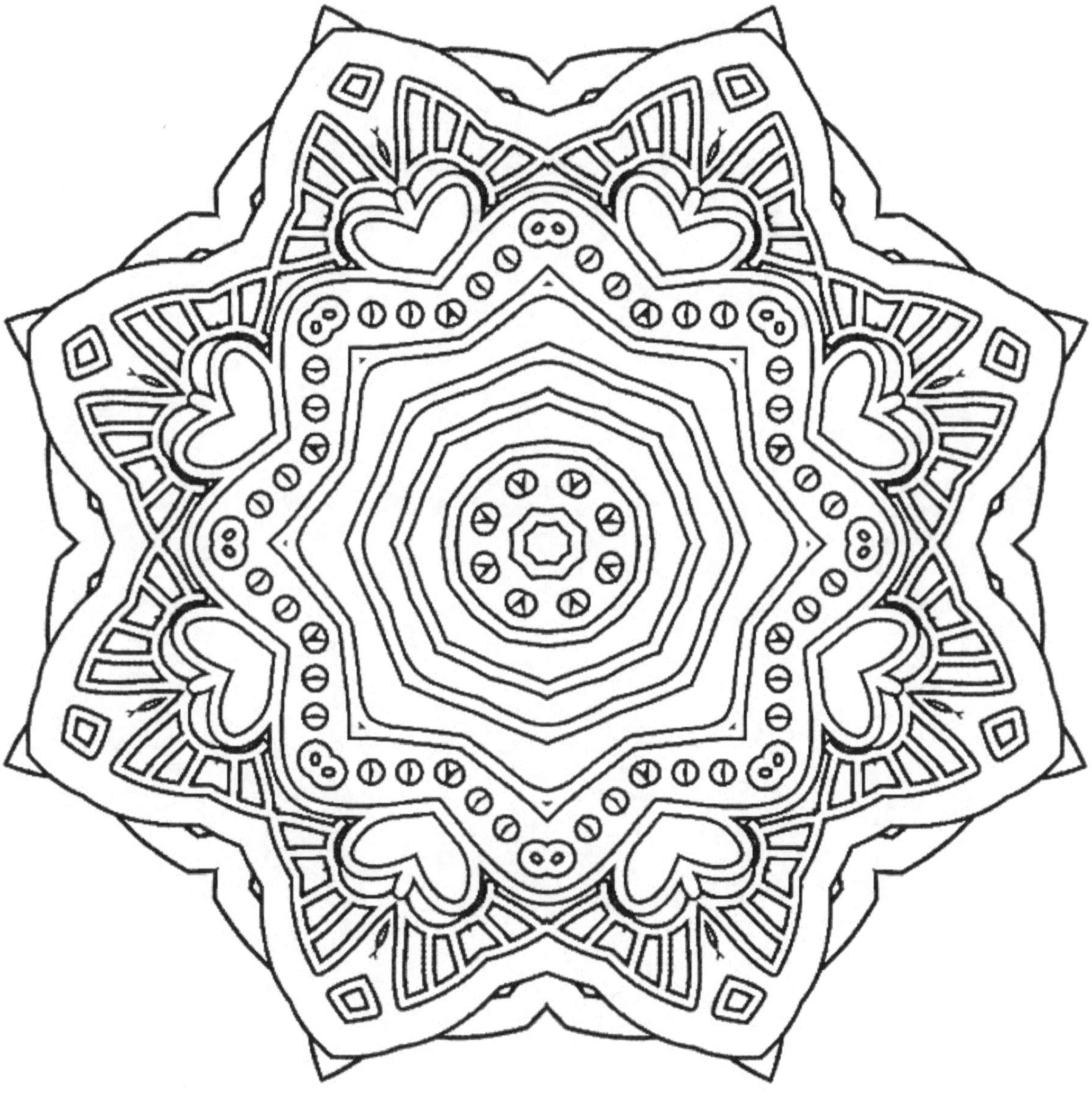

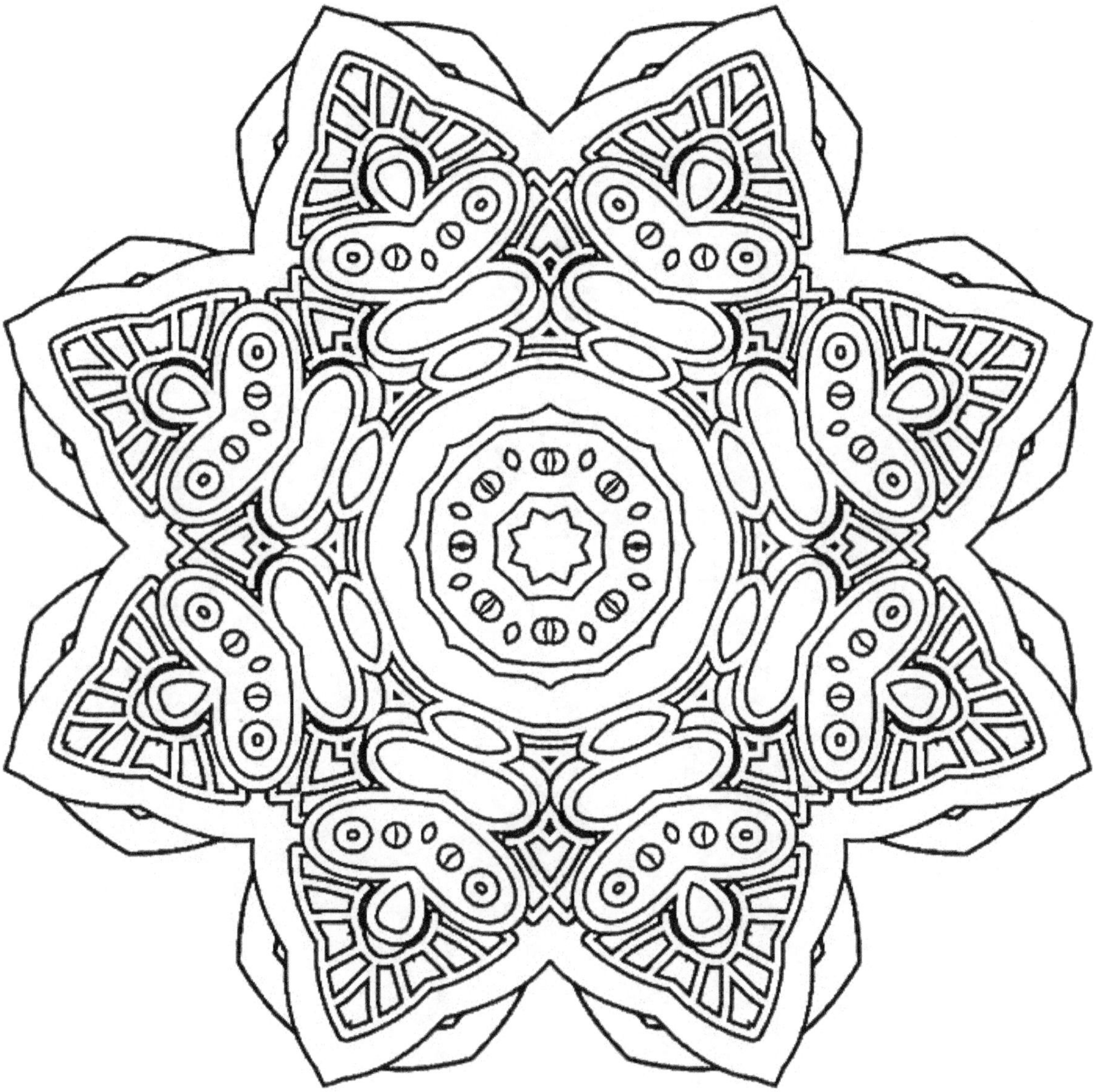

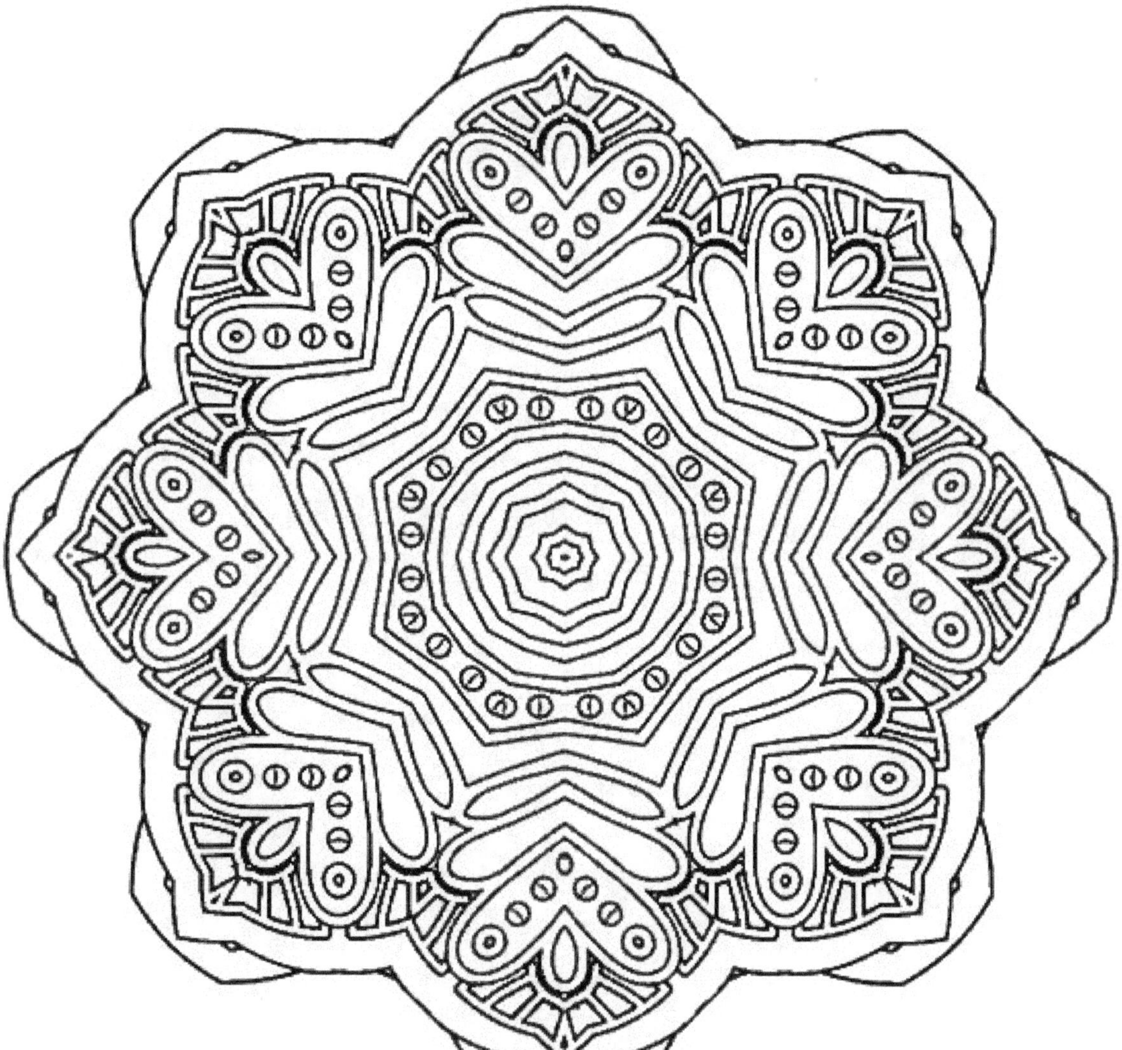

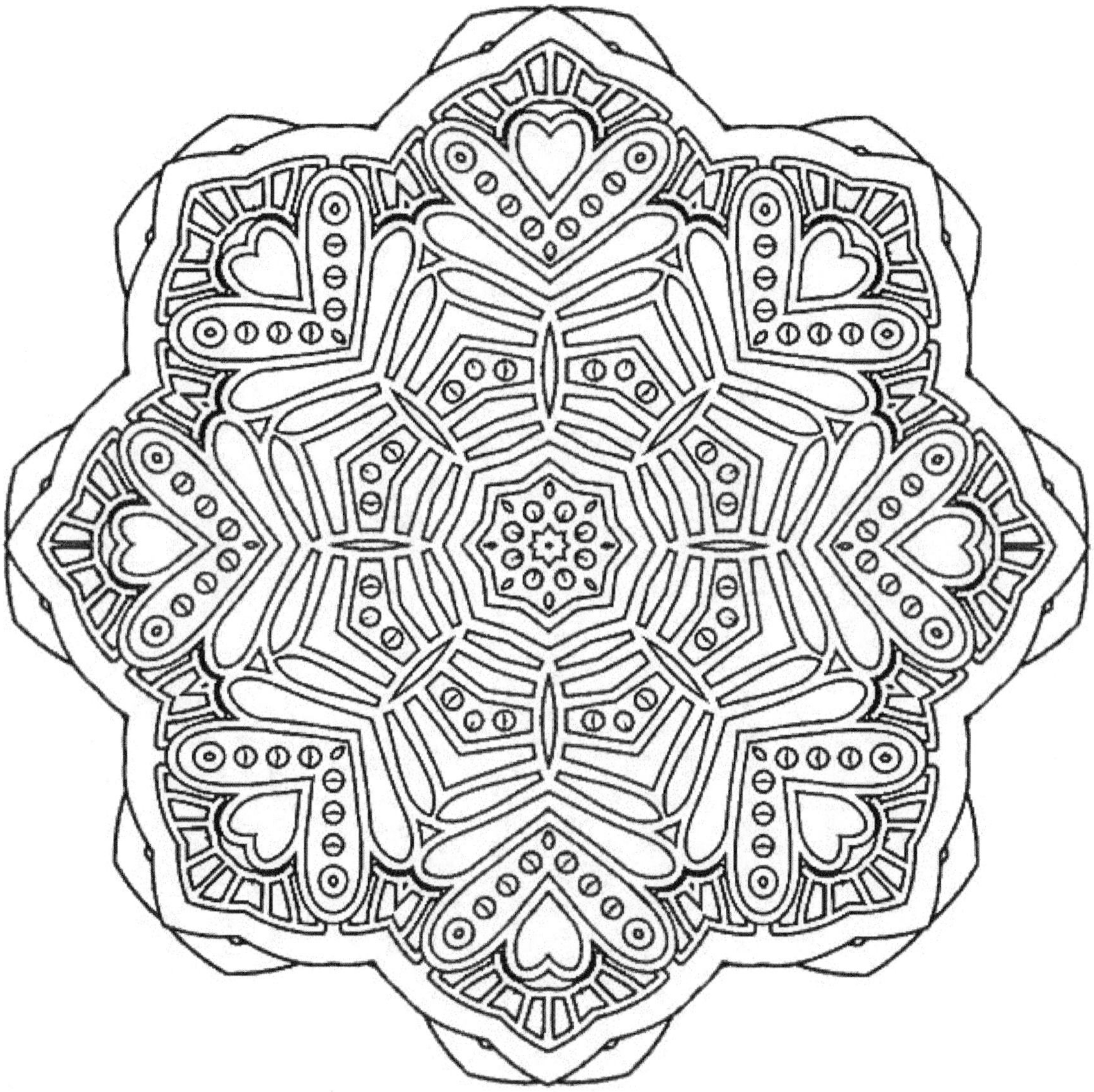

www.ingramcontent.com/pod-product-compliance
Lightning Source LLC
Chambersburg PA
CBHW080614190526
45169CB00007B/3009
9781534794498